My

Mindfulness Journal

To Write In

"Living 24 hours with mindfulness is more worthwhile than living 100 years without it." - Buddha

"Every morning we are born again. What we do today is what matters most." – Buddha

Start Your Journey Slow

HOW TO USE THIS JOURNAL

Mindfulness at the core is paying attention to our present moment and a wonderful tool we can have to practice mindfulness is a journal to write down all our thoughts and ideas. By keeping a mindfulness journal, we are liberating our minds from anxiety and we start paying attention to the details.

A journal can inspire our creative writing and can also connect us with the present. A journal for mindfulness can help us feel more present in our daily life and by following the prompts included in this journal we can release stressful feelings and experience the joy of being present in the moment.

Starting a mindfulness journal is a great practice for those who really want to appreciate the beautiful little things that life has to offer and to relieve stress and anxiety. All you need is to follow the prompts included in this journal to get started with your mindfulness journey. A great idea is to write down each and every day in your journal and then take the time to breathe and reconnect with nature by taking a walk while you pay attention to your surroundings.

The idea is that we start reconnecting with our own selves by being present in the moment and by writing down every thought that we have. Feel free to follow these prompts and the mindfulness quotes included in your journal but also feel free to write down everything that makes you feel grateful and present in the moment. Translate all your daily experiences into words and be as creative as you want and feel. This is your journal and you are free to write down all your beautiful thoughts and ideas.

Set aside a specific time each day to write on your mindfulness journal and make it a new habit to practice your creative writing. Ten minutes a day is all it takes to start practicing mindfulness with your new journal. Maybe you can decide to write in your journal after your yoga class or simply start writing every morning before everybody wakes up. The prompts included in this journal are designed to help you create that flow of writing and you will notice that once you start it will be easier and easier.

How to Practice Mindfulness

To start practicing mindfulness it is essential that we learn to focus our mind in the present moment. The reality is that the only place where we can completely be present is here and now. We must learn to train our mind to be in the now and to be present in this very moment that we are living now. Although we need to plan for the future and reflect on the past, we also need to find that beautiful balance that will make us appreciate the present moment we enjoy right now. This journal will be your tool to start writing all your present thoughts to help you keep your calm and your mental clarity.

Being mindful is also paying attention to your surroundings and being able to appreciate all the details without worrying about tomorrow or the past. Mindfulness can help us be more creative and more grateful for what we already have. Being mindful is also being able to relax and enjoy the moment and focusing on your thoughts, your breathing while listening to relaxing music. Make it a habit to listen to relaxing music every time you write on your mindfulness journal. At the core of mindfulness is the joy of paying attention to your present moment and what you are doing without regretting on the past and without worrying about the future.

Writing will always have a southing effect on our minds and writing all your thoughts inside this journal will help you with this southing process that will lead you to mindfulness. Writing on your mindfulness journal is one of the most powerful tools that you now have to practice mindfulness.

Writing is a creative act and one of the best ways to reconnect to your inner soul. You can start practicing awareness of your present moment just by writing about your surroundings and your observations and how you feel about it. As you move on with your mindfulness journaling practice you will start to notice a better attitude towards the world around you, you will start to feel more present.

To practice mindfulness, it is important that you acquire the habit of writing down in your journal all the details you see and feel around you and start translating all your experiences into words. Don't be afraid to be creative, in fact creativity is one of the amazing benefits of being mindful. The idea is to let that inner energy you possess reconnect with your surroundings while you feel present in the moment. Take a walk-through nature and start listening to the sounds of nature. Go to your favorite park with your journal and start observing with care and calm all the beauty that surrounds you.

Take a pause while you walk and breathe and feel the amazing beauty of that very moment. Then allow yourself sometime to reflect on what you are feeling and write it down in your journal.

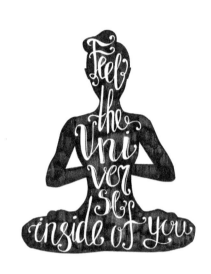

Practice meditation. Meditation is a very powerful tool you have to start feeling your present moment. Close your eyes and think about your blessings while you breath deeply. Write about all those tiny details you noticed during your day and appreciate the colors of nature in your mind. Listen to the world around you and let go all the stress that you may be carrying inside, think that all that matters are the now and the present moment. Do this exercise on a daily basis and register all your thoughts in your mindfulness journal with joy and with happiness. The goal is to encourage your self-love and to start practicing gratitude while you notice more and more all the beauty that each moment you have the privilege to breathe offers you.

Notice all your body sensations and try to let go all the negativity and the judgement while you reconnect with your inner soul and the outside energy that is always present around you. Try to understand those sensations and register them in your journal. Notice your emotions while you breathe and feel the present moment, everything you need is here with you, you will start to feel complete and grateful for what you already have.

Allow all your senses to reconnect with nature and with your creative energy, you are a part of that energy, we are all part of one beautiful and infinite positive energy. Feel it, write about it and feel the joy of being alive today in this very moment immerse in this beautiful energy called life.

I am conscious of my strengths, I am mindful of my abilities and my skills. What do I appreciate about myself?

I know I have the power to be present in the present moment, here and now. How do I feel about this moment?

I enjoy who I am. I am thankful for...

I am conscious and thankful of all the people that have helped me get where I am today. Who are the people that have helped me?

I am grateful for the inspiration and support from all the people I know

I am thankful for...

> *I am conscious and mindful of the shelter that I enjoy every day.*

I feel grateful for my beautiful home and the comfort it provides to me and my loved ones. I am thankful for...

I am aware of my wonderful work that provides food and shelter to me and those who I love. What do I love about my work?

> *I am mindful of all the good that my work produces for me and my loved ones.*

I love what I do, and I do what I love. I am thankful for...

I am feeling peaceful and I am feeling focused with my life and this very moment. I am grateful for...

I am happy with my life today and with the beautiful bed I have. My bed is a sacred place that I treasure

I feel good about my bed and my space to rest. Preparing for bed is always a ritual I enjoy. I am grateful for...

Today I feel peaceful, happy and connected with the universal energy. How I feel blessed today?

I know I am a part of this wonderful universe and my energy is in harmony with my surroundings and with nature. I am grateful for...

_____
_____
_____
_____
_____
_____
_____

Today I am supporting someone special to achieve a peaceful moment.

Today I spread peace and joy, so we can both connect with our present moment

Today it's a special day. I am grateful for...

Today I forgive and forget all the resentments of the past, today I can enjoy this beautiful moment in peace

Today I am grateful and happy. I am grateful for...

Today I am mindful for all the teachings I received in the past that have helped me get to this beautiful present moment I enjoy right now

I am grateful for...

Today I think about all my inner strengths and weaknesses.

Today I acknowledge and accept who I am with joy and happiness. I am grateful for...

Today is beautiful and special and today is unique. This beautiful day is here for me and for those who I love and respect.

This beautiful day is here and now for all of those who believe in the beauty and power of this very moment. I am grateful for...

Today I discovered my divinity and the power of my thoughts and words.

My actions and my thoughts today are focused on this very moment and I feel happy and blessed. I am grateful for...

Today I realize that I believe in myself and that all I need is right here with me in this unique and precious moment.

I thank the universe for being an active part of this beautiful energy I am feeling right now. I am grateful for...

Today I am open to change and positive transformation. I know my flows and my qualities.

I embrace change and all the possibilities that this beautiful moment is bringing to my life. I am grateful for...

Today I am feeling inspired and joyful about all my possibilities but above all I am feeling happy about being where I am.

I am finding the inspiration I need inside my soul and all around me right now.

I am feeling my own energy, I am listening to my soul. I am grateful for...

Today I choose to smile and to be happy.

There is no one or nothing that can ruin this beautiful moment because I know that my own happiness and wellbeing are already inside of me

I feel happy, I feel blessed. I am grateful for...

Today I think about all those beautiful things that make me feel happy

Today I think about all those beautiful people that have influenced my own existence with positive energy and joy.

I am grateful for...

Today I remember the child I am, and I embrace my playful and childhood behavior.

I know that I came to this world to be happy and joyful.

I know inside my soul I am still a child and I reconnect with my happy childhood mindset.

Don't Judge Your Thoughts and Your Feelings, Just Be Present in This Beautiful Moment

I am grateful for...

Today I think of all those people that have touched my life in a positive way and I thank them for being a part of my life. I am grateful for...

My favorite way to spend my day is…

The things that make me feel happy every day are...

The things that make me feel grateful are...

Take Notice of all the Blessings You Already Have

Why I feel today is important in my life...

The most precious moments of my life are...

I feel creative when I...

The feelings I appreciate the most in my life are...

What is the meaning of love to me...

"When you realize nothing is lacking, the whole world belongs to you." — *Lao Tzu*

What is the meaning of gratitude to me...

What are the most important people in my life and what are my feelings for them...

What are my most important qualities and virtues....

How do I feel about life…?

What makes me sad...

"We are awakened to the profound realization that the true path to liberation is to let go of everything." — Jack Kornfield

I can describe myself with these words...

What do I feel when I wake up to a new beautiful day...?

What have I learned from my mistakes…?

I feel happy and energized when...?

I describe my present emotions as…?

"Be happy in the moment, that's enough. Each moment is all we need, not more." — Mother Teresa

What do I need today...?

Mindfulness

What do I feel grateful for today...?

What can I do today and now to make this day special…?

What inspires me today…?

What is stopping me from being happy today...?

"Be kind whenever possible. It is always possible." — Dalai Lama

Have I made the right choices today for my life…?

What good habits I am developing today...?

How do I feel about my relationship with my loved ones today...?

How do I feel I am being perceived by those who love me...?

> *"The little things? The little moments? They aren't little."* – Jon Kabat-Zinn

> "Mindfulness is a way of befriending ourselves and our experience." – Jon Kabat-Zinn

> "Mindfulness means being awake. It means knowing what you are doing." – Jon Kabat-Zinn

> "Many people are alive but don't touch the miracle of being alive." – Thích Nhất Hạnh

___

___

___

___

___

___

___

"Each place is the right place--the place where I now am can be a sacred space." – *Ravi Ravindra*

> "Live the actual moment. Only this actual moment is life." – Thích Nhất Hạnh

> "When we get too caught up in the busyness of the world, we lose connection with one another – and ourselves." – Jack Kornfield

How do you describe your emotions today?

_____
_____
_____
_____
_____
_____
_____
_____
_____

> "Much of spiritual life is self-acceptance, maybe all of it." – Jack Kornfield

Where is my attention now?

_____
_____
_____
_____
_____
_____
_____

"Nothing ever goes away until it has taught us what we need to know." – Pema Chödrön

"Mindfulness isn't difficult, we just need to remember to do it." – Sharon Salzberg

> *"If you want to conquer the anxiety of life, live in the moment, live in the breath."* – Amit Ray

> *"What would it be like if I could accept life – accept this moment – exactly as it is?"* – Tara Brach

> "Looking at beauty in the world, is the first step of purifying the mind." – Amit Ray

"A few simple tips for life: feet on the ground, head to the skies, heart open…quiet mind." – Rasheed Ogunlaru

"Open the window of your mind. Allow the fresh air, new lights and new truths to enter." – Amit Ray

"A few simple tips for life: feet on the ground, head to the skies, heart open…quiet mind." – Rasheed Ogunlaru

"Peace comes from within. Do not seek it without." – Buddha

"Every experience, no matter how bad it seems, holds within it a blessing of some kind. The goal is to find it." – Buddha

> "Our life is shaped by our mind, for we become what we think." – Buddha

"Be where you are, otherwise you will miss your life." – Buddha

> "Every morning we are born again. What we do today is what matters most." – Buddha

Describe your feelings today and describe all the tiny details you noticed today

ENJOY EVERY MOMENT
here and now

> *"If you miss the present moment, you miss your appointment with life. That is very serious!"* - Thich Nhat Hanh

> *"Do every act of your life as though it were the last act of your life."* - Marcus Aurelius

"Emotion arises at the place where mind & body meet. It is the body's reaction to mind." - Eckhart Tolle

"Reality is only an agreement - today is always today." - Zen Proverb

"The significance is hiding in the insignificant. Appreciate everything." - Eckhart Tolle

"Be happy in the moment, that's enough. Each moment is all we need, not more." - Mother Teresa

"Mindfulness, the Root of Happiness" - Joseph Goldstein

HOW I FEEL TODAY MATTERS

> "I'm here to tell you that the path to peace is right there, when you want to get away." - Pema Chödrön

CPSIA information can be obtained
at www.ICGtesting.com
Printed in the USA
LVHW102344010419
612627LV00006B/90/P